Custom Classic Cars

D0968210

CUSTOM
CLASSIC
CARS

A BEGINNER'S GUIDE TO
RESTORING A VINTAGE VEHICLE

JON J. CARDWELL

Vayahiy Press

ANNISTON, ALABAMA

CUSTOM CLASSIC CARS
"A BEGINNERS GUIDE TO RESTORING A VINTAGE VEHICLE"

TABLE OF CONTENTS

CHAPTER ONE

CARS OF THE STARS
AND PLANES OF FAME

"America's love affair with the automobile" began quite a long time ago; in the 1960s according to Jeremy Hsu in an article he had written in the Scientific American™ and appearing online in May of 2012.[1] The term was coined by General Motors and used by TV personalities to psychologically move and motivate American audiences to make a purchase of their products.

They may very well be, but the automobile itself, is still generally fascinating for most people. When I was a young boy, just seven years old, I wanted to be a deep sea diver. To me, the world under the sea was as fascinating as walking on the moon itself... and with equipment that had only been around for decades (at the time). Undersea exploration was a new science, relatively speaking.

---

[1] http://www.scientificamerican.com/article.cfm?id=why-americas-love-affair-cars-no-accident

Likewise was the invention of the automobile. Modern diving and modern driving, though having some very primitive roots has really only been around for just over a century.

Although the psychology of making a new car purchase has continued in the American auto industry in much the same way; and quite possibly does have an effect upon those watching the advertisements, pulling them just over the edge in order to make a decision, the terminology employed wouldn't seem to have much bearing on the large number of people, not only in America, but all around the world, who have a love for old, vintage and classic cars.

When I was growing up in southern California, my dad or my uncle always had some kind of car project going on. I remember that when I was as young as 12 or 13, we would keep our eyes peeled for any kind of vehicle from the 1930s, like Ford's Model A, so that my dad and I could build and restore it.

I remember travelling an hour away on weekends to my aunt and uncle's home, and as soon as we got there, I'd run to the garage to see the 1934 Ford Graham my uncle was working on in his garage. I was fascinated by the wooden-spoke-wheels. I was awestruck by the straight-eight cylinder engine. I was jaw-slacked, mouth-opened, wide-eyed amazed over that vehicle, and I don't recall hearing Grouch Marx on the reruns of *You Bet Your Life* mention anything about "America's Love Affair."

When we moved to Riverside, California from San Pedro in 1971, my dad took us to "Cars of the Stars and Planes of Fame" in Chino, California, which was visible from the Riverside Freeway. To me, going there was better than going to Disneyland or the beach or any place I could think of.[2] All those old cars, those used in the movie... "Picture Cars" they called them. At that time, the sedan used in death scene of Warren Beatty and Faye Dunaway in *Bonnie and Clyde* was there. What a place for a kid like me. Wow.

Do you love old cars? Vintage cars? Classics? How about hot rods, custom cars, theme cars, funny cars, rail cars, stock cars or formula racers? You probably do. That's probably why you have this book.

I'll tell you, I loved them all. For a while, I think when I was six, I wanted a Lotus GT, and then the following week I probably saw something else and wanted that. When *Batman* (1966) came out as a movie and also as a TV series that same year, I definitely wanted that two-seater Ford Futura that was

---

[2] Wikipedia says that Cars of the Stars and Planes of Fame moved to Buena Park in 1971, near Knott's Berry Farm, probably right by Movieland Wax Museum. I have no doubt that the majority of it moved there, however, it wasn't 1971 because we didn't go there until 1972, because we in the summer of 1971.

converted into the Batmobile for Adam West. When they played *The Graduate* (1967) on TV (so it was edited), I wanted an Alfa Romeo. I watched the movie *Bullit* (1968) with Steve McQueen and wanted a Mustang. I saw the original *The Italian Job* (1969) and I wanted a Mini Cooper.

Could you imagine if you had any one of those cars, in whatever condition, and working on it, restoring it, and eventually driving it down the highway? It would be like driving around in art. Wouldn't it? That's exactly how I feel about it. I'm taking a spin around the block *in art*.

 **Vintage Cars: Some History**

Vintage cars are commonly regarded as the cars and automobiles that were produced at the start of the second decade of the 1900s and ended about a decade after, a good starting point for this era was when the First World War ended. When the era ended is a little unclear but many experts insist that it was in the end of 1930. That is why some vehicles produced after 1925, which some American vintage car experts say is the end of the era, are considered to be classic cars as well as vintage cars. There are also those that considered the end of the First World War and the start of the Second World War as the vintage car era.

Either way, the vintage car era was when many automotive experts, enthusiasts, and aficionados consider as one of the greatest eras in automotive history because many innovations were installed and more people could afford them. Before this era owning a car was near impossible and before the vintage era ended, numerous American families owned a car.

Many factors contributed to this upsurge in vehicle production. The economy was at an all time high, roads were being paved and the vehicles were becoming practical, convenient and affordable. Because cars were in great demand, many car companies were created and they all pushed for sales.

Yet because of the stiff competition and the overwhelming decline of the economy, which resulted in the great depression of 1929, many of these car companies folded and only about ten percent of them survived. Some of those that folded were small automotive companies that couldn't handle the unpaid bills and were producing subpar vehicles that couldn't withstand the test of time.

Ford, Hudson, Oldsmobile, Daimler, Dodge, Chrysler, and DeSoto were among the major companies that persevered. They were able to produce cars stamped with quality and durability that are still road worthy to this very day. These companies were able to produce vehicles and automobiles that were considered luxurious and highly durable. Automotive innovations such as car heating, in-dash radios, higher performance engines, and introduction of glycol-cooled radiators, allowed these cars to be used anywhere and anytime with premium passenger comfort.

Today, a number of these cars still exist and are still esteemed as highly reliable and road worthy modes of transportation. A number of car buffs regard vintage cars as the trophies of their collections and present them in car shows.

Some of these vintage cars have been salvaged from junk yards or from abandoned garages. So they weren't in the best of shape when found. One friend of mine found a "gem" in an old salvage yard guarded by nearly twenty Rottweiler, Doberman and German Shepherd dogs. He said it took him a couple of years to get the wet dog smell out of the interior of his Model A Ford (personally, I think he just got used to it or was in denial because I could still smell it; and I'm not so sure they didn't have a Saint Bernard or two in the mix also).

Whether you have to deal with a problem like that of my friend's, or just going through the step by step revival process, to restore these babies to their full glory is going to come with a pretty hefty price tag and cost a very pretty penny. If you have a vintage car that has numerous problems, looking for parts to restore them can become a problem in itself. Parts for vintage cars are hard to find and if you ever find one, they may be quite expensive.

But don't worry— be happy, as the song says. Because if you happen to find even an old junker and clunker of a vintage auto, you are weeks, months and even years ahead of the rest of us. Finding that car to restore is a major undertaking all by itself.

With some perseverance of the saints and the patience of Job, a vintage car restoration project will be its own reward. You've got yourself a vintage vehicle when there are not too many of them seen on the road these days. Whether it is running or not, you are the owner of a vintage car. Even when my uncle's Graham was in its worst condition, he was still king of the cars to us kids. And once your vintage project is fully restored, you have reason to be as proud as red rooster rolling up the hill in a green wagon (got that one from Mr. Haney on *Green Acres*).

 **Restoration versus Rebuilds**

There is a difference between auto restoration and rebuilds. A rebuilt car can contain any type of part. True restoration, consists of getting as much authenticity into the automobile as possible, right down to the hub caps and whitewalls. The car will only retain its value if it is restored to its original condition, not rebuilt into a different car. While "pimping your ride" may be popular at the moment, a restored car is supposed to take us back in time, not remind us of the present.

Yet, having said that, another part of history is not only the events surrounding the date, but it also includes the participating culture; that is, those individuals of that era involved. We must therefore also include vintage car customization, which allows the restorer to build the car in such a way that not only brings the vehicle to its time frame, it also restores it with a detailed finish using a number of "aftermarket" extras.

This would apply to many of your muscle cars in the 1960s and 1970s. Some of these restorations and refurbishments may not carry as high a value as the same car restored as near original as it can get; nevertheless, that's certainly not what this book is about. This book is about introducing you to a hobby for cars that you already love... and perhaps love so much that you choose to make a career of this. If it were all about the money, there are easier and less troublesome ways to make money.

The process of car restoration encompasses not only the parts of the car that can be seen by others, but also the mechanical components that go unseen. These are also restored or replaced as necessary, and ideally, to their original condition. Vintage car restoration is an art form unto itself. It takes people years to restore classic, vintage cars properly.

Vintage auto restoration involves the process of disassembling the entire car, cleaning and either replacing or repairing the original parts, and then putting the whole car back together again. In order for the car to maintain its original value, it must be restored with all of the proper parts. In most cases, the engine must be completely rebuilt.

A person who wants to restore a vintage automobile should first have his head examined. Typically, this is a racer who has suffered from one too many  head injuries in crashes and accidents on the track. Now, all kidding aside, I do say that because if you know anyone who has done a vintage restoration, a few of them may not attempt it again. It is a lot of hard work. Nevertheless, it is rewarding work... and to drive around in a car that you have restored yourself, there's nothing quite like it.

Mechanical knowledge is as important as doing body work to the car. In most automotive shops, body work and mechanical work are two different trades. Someone who wants to restore vintage cars has to know both aspects of car repair.

In addition, a car restoration includes the interior of the car. It is usually more desirable to repair the upholstery, if at all possible. You may not be able to get a replacement seat for a 1955 Chevy, but you can recover the seats using material that is very close to that used for a '55 Chevy.

A car that is merely replaced with lookalike parts has not been properly restored. A vintage car can be worth quite a bit of money to a collector if it has been carefully restored to its original condition. This usually means that you will have to do quite a bit of searching to find parts and paint for your car.

You will also want to use the original paint for the car, if possible. There are many different places where you can purchase the original car paint, or one very close to it. We will discuss places to purchase parts and accessories a bit later.

You need to have patience, time, space to work, and money in which to buy parts and materials. Most important of all, you must have a love for cars. If you love old cars and do not want to see them put to rest in the junk yard, this is your opportunity to give them a new lease on life. Although it can be costly, the restoration can be done over a period of time to accommodate your budget. You will need a place to work on the car and storage for the automobile when it is not in use.

There are businesses that practice the art of vintage car restoration. They can generally restore a vintage auto in much less time than you. Those who collect cars or do not have the time or inclination to work on the projects often send their cars to such businesses.

Money can also be made by learning how to restore vintage automobiles. Once you have successfully completed one restoration project, you may find you miss your hobby. There are those, like my uncle for example, who restore automobiles as a hobby throughout their lives. As they can only use so many cars, they often sell those they no longer want and make quite a profit.

 **Insurance Considerations**

Restoring a vintage car is a labor of love. While admittedly there are some that do this as a business, all of them, those that restore and collect vintage cars, are driven by their passion, they are fuelled by their desire for vintage cars, and watching their projects develop before their eyes and finally return to their full glory is what brings joy to the car restoration buff.

After restoring a vintage car, a lot of people would either drive out from time to time, or keep it in storage so that the vehicle will be in great condition when it is presented at car shows. This great concern for safety is understandable because a vintage car restoration project is no laughing matter. A huge investment in time, money and effort has been accomplished on your project, and watching the destruction of a car or to have it stolen can be a huge let down.

This is where having insurance comes in. Unlike regular car insurance, however, vintage car insurance can be quite different. One thing that collectors like is that vintage car insurance is far cheaper than regular car insurance, relatively speaking. That's because a vintage car is seldom driven.

Further, the price of a vintage car insurance policy will depend upon the make and model of the vehicle— the rarer the car, and the more expensive it is in the market, the higher the cost of the policy. You should make sure that your insurer will guarantee the highest value of your car prior to signing the policy (if you're under 18, you'll need your parents to sign with you in most cases). There have been some insurance companies who have denied claims for complete appraisal.

Custom Classic Cars

Having a guaranteed appraisal included in your policy will mean extra charges, yet this is a worthwhile investment as you are protected in the event that your car is stolen or is damaged beyond total repair.

Learning the ins and outs of insurance at an early age is something that will be useful for you with all your major purchases as you go on and grow up in life: a car, a house, a boat— whatever, they all need insurance.

Looking for vintage car insurance can be as simple as flipping through the yellow pages or browsing through vintage car magazines. In fact, if you do business with one of the more established companies, they will more than likely have supplements that include vintage, classic and collector vehicles. Most companies will be able to give you an estimated quote right over the phone when you provide them with the vehicle info. Comparison shop and get the best price you can. Remember, the money you save on insurance is money you can spend on your restoration project.

One of the more popular ways to find vintage car insurance is browsing the Internet. Here you will be able to find numerous insurance companies that can offer you some great deals. Moreover, you don't have to go to the physical location to get a quote. In a matter of minutes, you will be able to get quotes from different companies and compare them.

 **Many Things to All...**

In what we have covered in this opening chapter, we can see that vintage automobile restoration can be many things to many people: it is an art form for some; a hobby for those who love old cars; a lucrative business; an investment as a collectible. It may be all these things to you, or just one of them. What does it mean to you?

In the next chapter, "*ROUNDING UP YOUR RESOURCES*," we'll take a look at some of the preliminary items and tools you'll need prior to beginning your restoration project.

CHAPTER TWO
ROUNDING UP YOUR RESOURCES

Before embarking on your project, make sure that you have all of the right equipment. In addition to mechanical tools, such as a wrench set, a socket set, etc., you will also need body work equipment and protective gear and clothing for yourself.

Some of the items you should have on hand before beginning your project include the following:

- ☑ Rubber gloves
- ☑ Face mask
- ☑ Eye goggles
- ☑ Abrasive pads
- ☑ Electric drill
- ☑ Electric sander with different heads for sanding and buffing

☑ Glazing putty

☑ Car tape (masking tape is fine)

☑ Magnetic cloths

☑ Power paint sprayer

☑ Wax

☑ Primer

☑ Paint

Remember that it is just as important to protect yourself and your environment when you begin restoring your vintage car. Make sure that you wear goggles and a respirator, especially when sanding and painting.

In the next chapter, "*PLAN YOUR DRIVE AND DRIVE YOUR PLAN*," we'll take a laying out your overall plan for beginning such a huge project.

Chapter *THREE*

Plan Your Drive and Drive Your Plan

Do you know how to take a car apart and put it back together? What about an engine? Do you know where the interior parts of the car belong? Do you have a good understanding about how they work? What about the body of a car? Do you know how to strip the original paint off of a car? What about repainting a car? Do you know much about how to reupholster car seats?

These are just some of what you should know if you plan on restoring your vintage car. While it may seem daunting at first, you need to take the project and divide it up into manageable tasks. All of the information that you need to do this job can be found either in books or on the internet; and if you want to do it, you will learn it; and if you learn it, you will get it done.

In order to approach and complete a huge task you need to plan. As I mentioned earlier, I was a deep sea diver in the U.S. Navy for many years. As a diving supervisor we had a saying:

"Plan your dive and dive your plan." If you have a 400 ft., 2600 ton Fast Frigate grounded on the beach or a sunken Adams Class Destroyer that needs to be raised, those are both incredibly huge tasks. They require planning. Likewise, so does your restoration project.

There is an old riddle that asks, "How do you eat an elephant?" The answer: "One bite at a time." This is the best attitude to take when looking over the automobile that you are going to restore. Just take it one section at a time and learn as you go. Love for cars and the ability and desire to learn are all that you need.

Now, as I've already mentioned some good reasons to have a plan and stick to it, please allow me to express the serious nature of having a plan. I personally know of a small number of instances where a restoration project was begun without a plan and the vehicle was never completed and the whole project abandoned. Don't let that be you. Build your plan, apply your plan, fulfil your plan and finish your car.

 **Your Workplace**

Another thing that you will need to know is where you are planning on doing this work and where the car will be stored.

Custom Classic Cars

In most cases, the place is your own garage. The restoration will most likely take place in the garage as the car will not be able to be moved around during most of the process.

If you do not have a garage and plan to work on the restoration in the driveway of your home, make sure that it is okay with everyone concerned. In some neighborhoods, cars are not allowed to be displayed on blocks, which is how your car will be a good part of the time.

Things that you will need are basic mechanic's tools as well as a power stripper. As you continue with your project, you may need additional tools to work on the chassis. As some tools, such as a power sander, can be expensive to purchase, you can often rent them from auto stores or rental yards. It is also a good idea to network with other restoration experts so that you can not only learn tips, but also borrow tools.

If you're still in high school and your school has an auto shop, some shop teachers allow their students to bring in projects from home for extra credit. And typically, if the shop teacher and the administration allow it, the use of their tools will go along with the use of their facilities.

 **Your Manual**

Once you find out the type of car that you are planning on restoring, make sure that you find out everything about it. There are manuals put out on every car that is made. I highly recommend you get the repair manual for the exact model of car that you are restoring. And if they are not contained in the same volume, you'll want to get something called, "The Owner's Worksop Manual." Haynes Automotive Publications puts out a repair manual and a separate workshop manual on specific late model cars. These manuals may often turn up on eBay or other online auction. You may have the car, but chances are that you do not have the manual. You need to have it.

You will need to know how to rebuild an engine. This is a task unto itself, but can be learned through your repair manual simply by going online. If you have not taken any automotive courses in the mechanical workings of an automobile, this may be the time to do it, prior to beginning the restoration process.

 **Your Selection**

What type of car are you going to restore? There is a difference between restoring an old Model T and a muscle car from the

1960s or 70s. For one thing, parts are much easier to find for the later model cars than for what are considered "antiques." Your first project should be something a bit easier, selecting a car that does not cost you a lot of money. I might suggest not going for one of the rare vintage models at first; nevertheless, if one has fallen into your lap, by all means work on it. That's your project. Otherwise, search out one of the late model classics to be your very first project; or even something newer than that. As you get better at this craft, you will be able to move on to bigger projects.

The following is a list of what you need to know before embarking on a car restoration project of your own:

How much is the car worth? If the car is something that has been in the family for awhile and you want to restore it out of sentimental value, this is a good way to get started. While most of us think of vintage car restoration as typical "classic" cars that have held their value through the years, such as the Chevys from the 50s, other people seek to restore vintage cars that, although not valuable, hold fond memories for them.

 **Your Checklist**

These are things to keep in mind before restoring your vintage vehicle:

☐ Is the car solid? Some cars have decay in the floorboards, which would have to be replaced. If the floor has rotted through, it may cause for your entire vehicle to fall apart. Inspect the body and chassis condition before you make a purchase. You don't want to spend a lot of time and money on a project that is doomed for failure from the start. Get a body expert, or at least someone experienced with body work to look it over with you. Ask your expert questions and kindly ask them to point out problem areas for you. In most cases, whomever you get to go with you will be glad to help you and share their experience and expertise. Ask what would need to be replaced on the body and how much repairs of such a nature would cost. It may prove to be too costly.

☐ If you decide to buy a car to restore, be very cautious of "deals" you may be offered by those you do not know. Yes, devious scammers do not merely lurk on the Internet. The proverbial "Used Car Salesman" still exists today. Some cars are so decayed and rotting through that no one doing restoration wants to touch them. Again, if you must for your first project, do something simple just to get a feel of the craft.

Custom Classic Cars

☐ Make a precise list of everything that needs to be repaired and what needs to be replaced. Get something like a composition notebook that you can write everything down in (don't use a writing tablet or loose leaf notebook paper—sheets of paper can get lost; and in a composition notebook, even if you are not as organized in your notes, at least what you have written will be somewhere in the notebook).

☐ Take digital photos of your project inside and out. Catalog those photos in your composition notebook. Use your cell phone or a digital camera and then download them to your computer so that you can keep a running log of your repairs; and since you will be working section by section, and task by task, not only will this give you a record, it provides a continual reminder of what needs to be done. Even when you are not actually and physically working on your project, you can look at your photos.

☐ In your computer, keep a folder that is dedicated for your project. Create subfolders to keep your images separated. You should also use something like MS Notepad (if you use a PC) to transfer your notes from your composition notebook into files that can be read on your computer. Keep your eNotes with your appropriate and associated images. It seems redundant and repetitive, but this will help you to learn and remember. This process will help you quickly recall the details of each section and every task.

☐ Take a real good look at the chassis. Photo and catalog your findings. Inspect the floorboards carefully as a car floor is terribly expensive to replace. Pull up the carpet to inspect for rust on the metal. Ensure that no part of the floorboard has been rusted through. Oxidation is your car's enemy so rust is not your friend. Although you can sand and grind surface rust away, rust can literally eat away at every bit of metal on your car; and if it has already eaten through metal, do not purchase the vehicle if you haven't already done so.

☐ Figure out where you are going to get the parts for the restoration. On the very inside cover of your composition notebook, whether front or back it matters not as long as the page you are writing on is blank, write down every place you have researched to get particular parts. Start looking around online and in the area for vintage car parts. Thanks to the internet, you can find just about anything you need online. If your project is a more economical late model vehicle, you may be able to find authentic parts from salvage yards known as "Pick-A-Part" in some areas, which is where you search out the yard to find vehicle that is the same model as yours, and using the tools from your own toolbox that you brought with you, you take the part off of the vehicle in the yard, pay for it at an exceptionally reasonable price, and take it home to put into your project.

☐ Establish a budget. This will most likely be an ongoing project, so you may want to establish a monthly budget towards your vehicle restoration so things do not get too out of hand.

☐ Finally, and most importantly, realize that your first attempt at restoring a vintage car may not turn out looking like a brand new vehicle. Keep everything in perspective and remember that part of this is your learning process as well.

Just like a map that you've marked out for your cross-country journey, knowing where you will stop along the way, etc, you are taking steps by "*driving* your plan and planning your *drive.*" By having a grasp on what you need to do, an approximate cost of the project, and your final expectations for the project, you should be ready to begin!

In the next chapter, "*CAR, AUTO, HORSELESS CARRIAGE,*" we'll take a close look at the types of cars you can restore.

CHAPTER *FOUR*
CAR, AUTO, HORSELESS CARRIAGE

The value obviously varies according to the vintage car being restored. Restoring an antique car, such as Stanley Steamer, would require a lot more effort than restoring the 1974 Plymouth Valiant that has been sitting in a garage for years. Naturally, the Stanley Steamer would be worth a lot more money once restored.

Some of the more popular cars that are restored are those from the 1950s and 1960s. These cars have withstood the test of time and are very popular among collectors. Quite often, these vintage cars are referred to as "classic" cars, while others like a Stanley Steamer or a Model T Ford, are considered "antique" cars.

Among auto restoration buffs, cars are typically placed into groups. In one sense, they are all vintage autos if you take the word vintage and apply its literal meaning to the term. Vintage means that it reflects some period of time. The term "classic" may also be used, in one sense, to describe certain models within a group; however, you'll find that these are also groups in and of themselves.

You will want to be able to identify the different groups in auto restoration because the groups with which your project falls into will help you to have a ballpark estimate of how economical or expensive your vehicle project can run; yet, it will also give you an idea of what value you can attach to your car when the restorations are complete.

Your groups or categories entail more than just walking through automotive history an picking out the cultural and technical differences between today's modern car, the family automobile of the post World War II era, and the horseless carriage at automotive transportation's birth.

The most common cars that are being restored by private individuals today include the following groups: (1) Muscle Cars; (2) Antique Cars; (3) Classic Cars; and (4) Vintage Cars.

 **Muscle Cars**

Muscle cars describe high performance cars with V8 engines,

which were manufactured in the United States between 1964 and 1975. They were never called "muscle cars" back then, but simply referred to as "cars" or "supercars." The typical muscle car was extremely fast and often used for illegal drag racing on street. Most of the people who owned muscle cars were young men, like many of you reading this book.

Nearly every car manufacturer in America made a muscle car back then, producing over seventy-five different makes and models. They came in three sizes: mid-size, compact, and what was called a "pony car." Some of the most popular muscle cars coveted today include:

AMC HORNET ☆ AMC DUSTER
CHEVY MALIBU ☆ CHEVY NOVA
DODGE CHARGER ☆ DODGE DART
FORD FAIRLANE ☆ FORD MUSTANG
FORD TORINO ☆ MERCURY COUGAR
MERCURY CYCLONE ☆ PLMOUTH BARRACUDA
PLYMOUTH DUSTER ☆ PONTIAC GTO

This is obviously a brief list because I mentioned that there were over seventy-five makes and models.

Muscle cars are prized by collectors and these cars from the late 1960s and 1970s are often displayed in collector car shows across the country.

 **Antique Cars**

Antiques are usually classified as items that are over one hundred years old. Some people will tell you that antiques can be as little as fifty years old. The definition varies depending upon who is selling and who is telling.

Antique cars are not the same as classic cars or vintage cars. Antique cars usually refer to those made pre-World War II. The Ford Model T would be an excellent example of an antique car.

Very few people try to restore antique cars in their own garage. Antique cars are collected by people who generally have a lot of money and space to store them. They are highly desired and coveted by the wealthy.

You will often see antique cars in parades or special shows. They do not run fast on the roads and have to have a special "antiques" license in order to be allowed on the road. They are often put on display, but not used for practical purposes. In other words, you are not going to run daily errands with the old Model T.

Pre-World War I era vehicles often started using hand cranks. These have been replaced in later model cars by the modern key ignition. There are very few true antique cars around today and those that remain are extremely valuable. If you are fortunate to be able to get your hands on a pre-WWII car, you may want to have a couple of projects under your belt before you begin to restore that one yourself.

If restored properly, an antique car can sell for hundreds of thousands of dollars to a collector.

 Classic Cars

You will often see examples of restored classic cars when you go to outdoor auto shows, which take place in the late spring to early autumn, but most typically in the summer in most parts of the country. People are eager to show off their fully restored classic cars to the general public. The Classic Car Club of America is an organization that many classic car restoration buffs join.

The original rules of the Classic Car Club of America stated that the car had to be manufactured between 1925 and 1948. The rules have relaxed somewhat over the years and the timeline isn't that strictly enforced. Many consider a car as "classic" that is twenty-five years old or more.

Depending upon the group you join, you may or may not be able to exhibit your 1970s muscle car. Many of the classic car clubs only exhibit the cars from the 1950s and early 1960s.

 They are popular among collectors and, if properly restored, driveable.

According to some of the experts, a classic car has to have the following qualities in order for it to be deemed a true classic:

➢ Must be built within the time period

➢ Must have been a high-priced, luxury auto when built

Strict classic car enthusiasts will maintain that by 1948, classic cars had virtually stopped existing. Mass production of automobiles was well on its way by that time and cars were generally affordable for just about anyone. The days of the luxury classic car ended shortly before the 1950s.

 **Vintage Cars**

According to the Classic Car Club of America, vintage cars are those that were built before 1930 and after the end of World

War I. Cars built before WWI are called "Veteran Cars" or "Veteran Era" cars. Many of the veteran era cars used a tiller to steer the vehicle rather than a steering wheel.

Most people today refer to "vintage cars" as an older car. Cars from the 1950s, 1960s and even the 1970s are commonly referred to as "vintage cars." These are the cars that are most popular with those who seek to restore cars on their own.

The cars from the 1950s are especially popular with collectors and restoration experts and are shown in exhibitions across the country.

 Precautionary Tips

No matter what type of car you are planning on restoring, here are some tips for you that may help to avoid some headaches and heartache:

- ✓ Set your pay-price for your restoration vehicle. If it's set at say, $1500, then don't go beyond that. If you can get one for less, great, but you want to avoid paying more than you know you can afford. This is your first project so you do not want break your bank on it.
- ✓ Check the car out thoroughly before agreeing to the

deal.

✓ Once restored, register the car with the Antique Car Association for a special license plate if it has been made prior to 1948.

✓ Ensure you have a safe and warm place to store the car when you are not working on it. It should be temperature controlled during the winter months.

Restoring any type of car, whether classic, vintage, antique, veteran, a muscle car, or that Olds Vista Cruiser station wagon that's just been in the family for years, takes basically the same type of knowledge. As parts are more difficult and expensive to get for the truly old cars, such as a 1925 Ford, it sometimes makes better sense for the home vintage car restorer to work on those that are a lot less costly to both purchase and restore. You're young and you've got plenty of time for plenty of other projects that are more elaborate and more expensive... but then, you'll have the know-how and experience to deal with it.

In the next chapter, "*THAT NEW CAR SMELL*," we'll embark upon restoring your vehicle's interior.

CHAPTER *FIVE*
THAT NEW CAR SMELL

Have you ever been on a car lot while your parents were shopping for a new car? Or perhaps you have been to the car lots, even before you turned driving age, and you've poked around the brand new models; do you remember that new car smell? The interior was so pristine that the odor of another human being had not yet changed that just-off-the-assembly-line new car smell. Now, you will probably not get that smell for the interior of your project without some artificial aerosol sprayed once you've reassembled your car, but you can keep that smell in mind while you're working.

Once you have looked over the car and you're satisfied with your "drive plan," begin with the car's interior. Take out the seats and pull up the carpeting on the floor, assuming that there is carpeting on the floor.

 **Floor and Seats**

The upholstery may be salvageable. Reupholstering a car seat can take quite a bit of work and shouldn't be done haphazardly. You want the same type of material that was used in the original upholstery, whether it is vinyl, fabric or leather. In most cases, you will need vinyl.

Chances are that the padding under the seat will also need to be replaced. Padding and vinyl can be purchased at any good, local fabric store. This store is where you can also get the tools you need to reupholster the seats.

If you need vinyl cords, you may be able to purchase them online or in a store that specializes in upholstery products. After you have removed the upholstery and padding, you should clean the seat, remove any rust, and also check the springs. If the springs are rusty or rotted, they should be replaced.

Once the seat is taken apart, the metal cleaned of any rust, bad springs replaced, you can then begin to replace the padding and the vinyl. There are many different methods when it comes to upholstering car seats. This is normally done with small nails that are covered up by cording. Unlike furniture upholstering, which uses ordinate studs, car seat upholstering is sleek, and less elaborate. The most important thing to remember is that you will have to make sure that the material is very tight over the frame before beginning to attach it to the seat.

The seats should be set aside and the car's floor inspected for any rust. Although you may have done a preliminary inspection when you purchased your vehicle, when you inspect the floorboards this time, make sure your workspace is well lit. I recommend that you use a hanging shop light. You want to be able to detect the very least bit of rust. Don't use a flashlight. It's just not bright enough. Use good shop light with at least a 60 watt bulb; a 100 watt bulb if possible.

Use a sandblaster to clear away any rust. As mentioned earlier in the book, if the floor is rotted through, you will need to replace the entire floor. The only times I would expend the  effort with a vehicle that has holes in the floor from rust is if the vehicle is quite valuable or if the car was given to me (so I that would mean no expense to me). A rotten floor is usually an indication that there are other problems elsewhere, such as a rusted gas tank, weak suspension with metal fatigue in the chassis, etc. Keep a careful eye out for other areas that may have suffered from oxidation. We must have oxygen to live, but it is also oxygen that eats up metal.

Once the floor has been cleaned, the new carpet can be installed. This is not difficult and carpet remnants can be picked up relatively inexpensively. Nonetheless, you will want to match the original carpet with the new carpet as close as possible.

 **Dashboard and Steering Wheel**

While working on the interior you need to take a good look at the dashboard and steering wheel. Make a careful inspection under the dashboard and take note of what is working and what is not. You may have to replace many of the electrical items here. This entire area will need to be cleaned and rewired. Replace dashboard parts as necessary from parts purchased online, through catalogs, at an automotive store or supply house, or from a salvage yard that happens to have your project's very make and model.

Take the dashboard apart and clean everything thoroughly. This is where the exploded view diagrams from your manuals will come in handy. The exploded view diagrams will help you to identify all the parts that should be in your dash, and in the case of wear, deterioration or an inoperative part, the piece may be more easily identified. Don't forget to take photos and jot down notes in your composition notebook.

In some cases, the plastic covering the dashboard may be cracked. Depending on the age of the car, this may be glass. This is relatively simple to fix. Plastic and glass can be cut to measure for the dashboard at a glass company or a hardware store. Make sure that you replace the cover of the dashboard with what was used in the original car.

All instruments on the dashboard should be cleaned and all rust removed, if any. Replace all instruments that are beyond repair. Although it is preferable to have an original replacement part, if you cannot get an original, you can use a similar model from the same time period.

Pay particular attention to the steering column when removing the steering wheel. In some models, there are shims that keep the column tight and the steering snug.

 **Trunk and Glove Compartment**

Pull out the carpeting from the trunk and inspect the metal of the trunk just as you did for the floor. The entire interior of the car should be spotless, as if it came out of the showroom, and this includes the trunk area.

Likewise with the glove compartment; inspect it, clean it, and restore even the smallest part that requires replacement.

The interior of the restoration is just as important as the exterior so complete this task with efficient care.

If you are working on this project during the evenings or on the weekends, this may take a month or two to get it right. Don't get impatient. Take your time and keep considering that new car smell. In the end, you want your interior to shine like new.

Once you've finished reinstalling the carpet, the dash and putting all the components of the interior back into place, keep the seats out until you are close to completing your project. Cover them with plastic and set them aside in a safe place.

Some Pointers

 The importance of belonging to a club when you are starting a hobby like this cannot be stressed enough. Club members will be eager to help you try to find places to get parts. It is best to have as many options open to you when it comes to finding part replacements, and having likeminded friends in a car club will certainly be beneficial.

Consider all the local salvage yards in your area. Check them out and see if you don't get lucky with a vehicle that is your exact make and model. Get acquainted with the owner or yard supervisor. Ask them if they can help you out by giving you a call if a car with your specs comes in. A couple of friends of mine had the good fortune of finding a duplicate model in the salvage yard, and by purchasing the cars from the yards, they were able to completely restore their project autos at a fraction of the cost.

Upholstery is not an easy craft to just "take up." If the upholstery on the car is in halfway decent condition and is not ripped, try cleaning it with an upholstery cleaning solution. There are even companies that provide this service.

It is still a good idea, however, to remove the covering and inspect the padding and springs of the seat, especially if the car is over 25 years old. It will probably be easier to cover the seat with the old upholstery. It will be more authentic, cheaper than buying new vinyl or fabric, and easier to stretch the intact original upholstery than to start from scratch and stretch the new material.

In the next chapter, *"NO BODY 'TIL SOMEBODY LOVES YOU,"* we'll discuss restoring your vehicle's body.

CHAPTER SIX

No Body 'Til Somebody Loves You

In most restoration projects, the car's body usually requires the most work. Yet, since the body is the first thing that people are going to notice, you're going to want to give it considerable attention.

Although there are some exceptions the car's body is made of metal. Take it apart one piece at a time and remove any and all rust. More than likely, you will need to strip it and repaint the parts.

Take this one step at a time. After covering the interior with plastic, you can remove the hood of the car, the roof, the trunk and the doors.

Clean everything thoroughly and remove all rust from both the inside of your parts and the outside. Removing the trim panels from the doors and inspecting for rust is extremely important.

Hidden rust in places like the access holes of the doors can be most treacherous because, although it will deteriorate more slowly, when it is finally noticeable, it may be too late to repair. And a note of caution here: if there is rust inside the access holes of the door for instance, that may be an indication there is a bigger problem elsewhere because those areas are typically not exposed to weather. So keep an eye on that.

It is very important, at this point, to inspect the frame of the car to make sure that it is straight. If the frame is damaged, it is more cost effective to replace the part that's damaged than to try to straighten it out, unless you have a body shop; and even then, I don't believe I've ever heard of anyone having any real success straightening a damaged frame. No, that doesn't mean that it isn't done. It's done all the time, but the best frame straightening will leave a car flawed. The best front end alignment will never really true your car. Once metal is bent and then bent back into place as a corrective measure, it is never the same; and anything that has to do with the chassis or the frame is structural, which means that it will never be absolutely factory true through repair. For the chassis, that means alignment problems. For the frame of the body, it means sealing problems. But in car restoration, you have to deal with that from time to time.

Much of what you decide to replace or repair will depend on

your skills and the equipment at your disposal. If you are replacing certain panels of the car, this will require welding it back onto the frame.

Sandblasting is the easiest way to remove the exterior paint. It can remove the surface rust as well and leave your metal ready to prep and repaint. Sandblasting equipment can be expensive to purchase, but can be rented at a more reasonable daily rate at some rental yard or outlet.

 Dents and Dings

Once you have the car completely sandblasted, it must be buffed and smoothed. Again, inspect for dents as they will be very apparent when the car is repainted. The buffing and smoothing of the car is time consuming, but is necessary for the body of the car to look like it just came off the showroom floor. The process is not one that is done overnight, but can be accomplished in a weekend.

Allow me to illustrate how important smoothing out the body is... as well the importance of your paint selection.

When I was a diver stationed in Hawaii, I bought an old beat up 1969 Ford Mustang, 3-speed, straight 6-cylinder. I bought it at a used car lot for $600 cash in 1987. It ran but it was the ugliest looking Mustang you ever saw. I'd been riding a Cannondale racing bicycle around the island and I just wanted to have a vehicle to get around in. After about six months or so of driving around, one of the other sailors stationed at Mobile Diving and Salvage Unit One mentioned to me that he really liked the Mustang. Before you know it, we were exchanging titles. He got my Mustang and I got his 1974 Plymouth Valiant (we both thought we made out on the deal). Anyway, to shorten this long story a bit, he got the Mustang running like a top and painted it midnight blue. Sadly, you could see every ding, dent, wave and weave in the body. The paint he used made it that much more noticeable but it was so pitiful many of the waves and dents would have shown up with nearly any good paint job.

So, take care with your car's body.

When all of the metal parts of the car have been removed of rust, paint and any dents or dings, and the surface has been buffed smooth, it is time to spray primer on the car.

Before priming, do this first. You don't want to leave metal flakes and particulates from the sanding job on the metal. That will attract rust much quicker than usual. Take these two steps and your metal will be ready for primer. (1) Use a microfiber cloth to go over the metal. Some call it a "magnetic cloth" but it is basically a fine, microfiber dusting cloth that will pick up that fine metal dust that is left as residue on the surface of your work and will not leave its own traces of lint and material behind; and after that, (2) Use a manufacturer's recommended solvent on the metal to ensure your surface is free of moisture. For the solvent, it should be one that will evaporate quickly to remove all moisture, but one with a base that will not conflict with your primers and paints. Certain acetones may leave a chemical residue that may cause adherence problems for older paints used on some vintage and antique autos. The most important thing about this is removing any possible moisture that can cause rust.

There are also rust inhibitors but that tends to lead to some controversy among some restoration aficionados. The purists insist that if an inhibitor was never used, it should not be used for authentic restoration. Other enthusiasts suggest that it's the preservation of the car, its culture and its era that is important, so the use of an inhibitor is not only allowed, but should be used to preserve the vehicle as an historical monument. Still others may say that it depends upon the project. You will have to decide what the best avenue is for you.

 **Prime and Paint**

Painting a car requires a power sprayer that is used for automobiles; and in most cases, this is done in a special warehouse since the fumes are toxic. I strongly urge you not to do it in your own garage if at all possible because most garages just don't have enough room or sufficient ventilation; but if you must, ensure that you rig plenty of ventilation support and wear a mask to prevent breathing in the toxic fumes from either the primer or the paint.

Auto paint is highly concentrated oil based paint and its special base is what gives the car its shine. A primer must be used before the car can be painted. The primer adheres to the metal and the paint sticks to the primer. The paint, by itself, will not stay on the metal without primer.

Spraying is necessary for an even coat. Use a high pressure paint sprayer to complete this job so that it doesn't have an amateurish look (like the flat orange paint on my Mustang when I bought it off the lot). You have probably noticed some cars on the street that look as if they have had a paint job done in their garage, or in the Kindergarten finger painting hour. You want to avoid this look.

The paint should be as close to the original color of the car as you can get. Paint colors change each year and it could be possible the paint that once adorned your car is no longer available from the manufacturer. Your manual will give you the information on the brand and color of paint needed for your car. Once you have discovered this, call the manufacturer of the paint and see if they still have it. If they do not still have the color, they can probably recommend a close matching color.

There are places online that can match the color of paint for your car to that of the original color. Save a paint chip and shop around. There are only three primary colors in paint and two pigments. The original paint used on your car consists of a mixture of these materials.

Some Pointers

 Use the same brand paint originally used on the car (such as PPG or DuPont). Not all paints are equal or alike and you want to get either an exact match or as close to it as possible.

 Of course, prior to painting your car parts, you will want to remove the tires, cover the interior, the trunk area, and under the hood. Make sure that each part is in good condition. The doors should be working well and the interior of the doors should be cleaned.

The windows should roll up and down easily. When painting the panels, make sure that you paint only the panels and not other parts of the car.

After priming and painting, you will also have to use a sealer. The technique of painting a car is one that takes quite some time and requires several coats of paint. In between coats, the panels are buffed. This is what gives the car that ultimate shine. Once the sealer is has been put on the car, let the vehicle sit and dry for at least 72 hours.

Working on the exterior of the car is the most time consuming of the entire vintage car restoration project. It is also the most rewarding. In order to make sure that you do things properly, use the best equipment you can find. You shouldn't cut corners on a restoration project, but most especially when working on the exterior.

Car restoration is an exciting art, but should be done correctly or else all of your efforts will be a waste of time.

In the next chapter, "*MORE THAN JUST BAILING WIRE*," we'll take a look at mechanical side of the restoration process.

CHAPTER SEVEN
MORE THAN JUST BAILING WIRE

I've got to tell you this one. Do you remember that '69 Mustang I told you about in the last chapter? Even though it was a mighty Ford Mustang, it was such a clunker that the universal joint broke off while I was driving on Interstate H2 near Schofield Army Barracks on my way to Wahaiwa. I knew I had to change it soon because I could hear the "clunk" every time I shifted gears. Thankfully, I had some bailing wire in my trunk (never mind why it was back there), and I got up under the car and used bailing wire to attach the drive shaft to the transmission via the busted u-joint. The bailing wire got me to Wahaiwa, to a parts store to buy a u-joint, and it kept me running for about a week (we had a lot of diving jobs from sunup to sundown and I couldn't get away to work on the car). Bailing wire can work in an emergency, but we definitely will not be using any of it on your project.

You've worked on your interior. You've worked on your body.

Now it's time to work on the mechanical side of your project, including your engine. Unless you want to put the car back together and tow it around, you're going to want it to start when you turn it over and move when you put it in gear. If you know something about how a car works, you will be able to accomplish this relatively simply. If not, now is a really good time to learn.

Begin by taking apart the engine and cleaning every part. All of the mechanical parts and wires that are under the hood (or in the trunk in the case of a Volkswagen Beetle), must be taken out and cleaned.

The engine has to be rebuilt. All of the components that make the engine run, keep it running, or assist in some process of running— the starter, alternator, radiator, carburetor, distributor, etc., should be rebuilt to the manufacturer's specifications; and these specs you'll get from your manuals and online resources.

I know I'm sounding like the congressman's parrot at the Department of Redundancy Dept., but it is preferred that you use original parts if you must replace any parts in your engine or on anything requiring replacement on the mechanical side, such as shocks, brakes, track bar, etc. And once again, take your photos, record your parts in your composition notebook, and at the end of your workday, transfer you images and information to your computer. If you need replacement parts, make a list on one page and try to get them, either all at once, or get them one at a time, placing a check mark on the page of your list when you have found and purchased the part. Leave a page blank opposite your list so you can write down any leads for the part that needs replacement. If you have more than one page of replacement parts for your notebook, then skip every other page whenever you start a new page for the replacement parts you need.

The other mechanical parts will have to be taken apart and cleaned. Some parts may be easy to clean and repair and have a longer lasting life. Check the belts, gears, any worn bearings, oil pump and the transmission. All of the moving parts should be cleaned thoroughly and restored to manufacturer specifications.

Personally, with regard to belts, since my engine is taken apart, I replace the belts, every one of them. Even if the belt appears to be in good condition, I replace it. If it is good, you can always use the old one as a spare in an emergency. Some hairline cracks in an older belt that has been sitting for a while may turn into a severe tear tomorrow, and then turn into a broken belt the day after that.

If you have experience with auto mechanics, this part of the restoration process will be time consuming, but not difficult. If you do not have vast mechanical skills, however, this will be a very difficult and crucial part of the project. Mechanical car parts are not cheap and to spend money on them only to not have it work, can be frustrating and expensive.

In addition to getting the engine in good working order, you want it to look as clean as possible. During the course of most car shows, the hood is opened and people take a look at the engine. You not only want the engine to work, but you want it to shine as well.

The fumes from chemicals and solvents to clean the grease and oil that accumulates in the engine chassis can be toxic. Wear protective clothing when you work: gloves, mask, goggles, etc.

Some Pointers

Most of the older cars have a manual transmission and a gearshift instead of an automatic transmission. Be sure that you understand how to work on a manual transmission when you begin your project.

Remember that working on the mechanical aspect of the job, although messy, is just as important as the body of the car. Although you may feel that "no one sees it," if you want to restore a vintage automobile the right way, you will take just as much time on the engine and mechanical components as you will the exterior of the car.

In the next chapter, "*DON'T FORGET THE DETAILS*," we'll take a look at restoring the accessories and giving attention to the little details that make your project stand out from merely a repair or simple rebuild.

CHAPTER EIGHT
DON'T FORGET THE DETAILS

The accessories of the car may be the last thing that you work on when restoring your vintage car. The accessories include the chrome bumpers, mirrors, tail lights, tires and hub caps. Like everything else, they should be restored to pristine condition.

All chrome accessories should be removed and polished to a high shine. Chrome is not difficult to polish. You can use just about anything on the market to polish chrome.

You also need to ensure that you straighten out any dents in the bumpers. This can be done by knocking them out from the back with a soft hammer. Many of the bodywork tools, some of them probably shown in one of your manuals, can typically be used for this. Although the dents on a chrome bumper are not as easily noticed as the dents and waves of the body of a car painted midnight blue, a noticeable dent or ding will detract from your auto's beauty. Sometimes the chrome plating has been damaged. If the bumpers are in good shape otherwise, in other words, no dents or dings, it may be worth it to have new chrome plating for your bumpers. Unless you have experience in this area, you will want to send the bumpers out to have it done for you (and that goes for all your chrome parts).

If the bumper is too far gone, you may want to replace it altogether. Remember that your goal is to get the car to look exactly as it did when it rolled off the original assembly line. You may have to do some shopping for a chrome bumper to match the make, model and year of your car. It will be well worth the effort when you consider that this is one thing that people tend to notice about cars.

Make sure that all of the fine details on the chrome bumper meet factory specs. The polished and completed chrome bumpers can be put aside in plastic until it is time to reassemble the car.

Other accessories include rear view mirrors and side mirrors. Again, make sure that they are the right mirrors for the right car. In most cases, you can use the same mirrors with some cleaning. If they are plastic, just clean them. If the mirror glass is cracked or rusty, have it replaced. If painted, they should be repainted with the same paint as the color of the car.

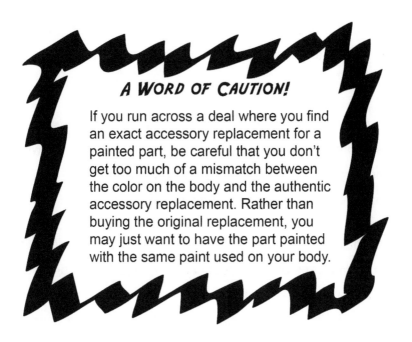

A WORD OF CAUTION!

If you run across a deal where you find an exact accessory replacement for a painted part, be careful that you don't get too much of a mismatch between the color on the body and the authentic accessory replacement. Rather than buying the original replacement, you may just want to have the part painted with the same paint used on your body.

The tail lights may be cracked or not working. Rewiring the tail lights to work should be no problem, but getting the actual tail light of a 1956 Chevy, for example, may take some effort. In some cases, the frame of the tail light can be salvaged and just the glass or plastic need be replaced. This is more cost effective and easier than trying to track down an exact match for the entire light fixture.

The grill on the front of the car must also be taken off and cleaned. If it is chrome, as many grills are on vintage cars, you will want to do for it as you did your bumper.

Tires will have to be replaced. You want as close to the same make and model of the year that the car was built. Find out what kind of tires were used for your car and get them matched as close as possible.

If you still have the original hubcaps, that's about as sweet as it gets. Sometimes hubcaps just appear out of nowhere when you're not looking; and when you have three and need a fourth, it might seem like you'll never find it (been there and done that).

More than likely you do not have all of the original hubcaps for the car. Hubcaps are the most common objects that are either stolen from the car or lost when the car runs over a large pothole. Again, find out what type of hubcaps were used for your car and look for them.

Hubcaps, another chrome part, can be polished up and made to really sparkle. Resist all urges to get "new and improved" hubcaps for the tires.

Of course, an exception to this is if your restoration project happens to be an aftermarket retro-restoration. An example of this might be a customized restoration of a muscle car, a 1971 Plymouth Roadrunner say, which is using aftermarket parts.

Now the aftermarket parts would be those available in 1971, such as wide tires, mag wheels, chrome valve covers, etc. What you want to pay particular attention to is getting the accessories that were available in 1971, not that were just made available today.

And an exception even to this, at least as some of the restoration enthusiasts go, is to use aftermarket parts that are a few years older to capture the era. For example, if you have a 1957 Chevy that is customized, and even super-charged, with parts from 1962 or whatever year and era you're trying to capture, some folks find this acceptable. Funny; many cite the movie *American Graffiti* (1973) as reference. Thank you, George Lucas.

A Quick Pointer

Try your best to restore your car to its original condition by using authentic parts. If this is not possible, use parts that are so similar that only the trained and experienced eye can detect it.

In the next chapter, "*FOR WANT OF A FUSE*," we'll take a look at restoring your vehicle's electrical system.

CHAPTER *NINE*

FOR WANT OF A FUSE

There is a very old saying that was coined by an old puritan minister in England some five hundred years ago. A variation of it goes like this: "For want of a nail the war was lost." That's what it was boiled down to from a decline of incidents, which began with the lack of a nail in a horseshoe— for the lack of a nail the shoe was lost; for lack of a shoe the gait of the horse was lost; for lack of the trot, the rider was throne; for lack of the rider the battle was routed; for defeat in the battle, the war was lost. That seems to be the basic thought behind the entire saying. Interestingly, this saying may readily apply to nearly every  aspect of your car restoration project. If you are off on just one point, it can mean the success of failure of the whole enchilada.

As for the electrical system, however, you need not have this step by step decline of events to produce failure. One blown fuse, one broken wire, or one faulty connection could keep your car from starting; so be very careful here.

It is a pretty good bet that the radio and the clock that are on the dashboard of your car do not work. The old analog clock, if your car has a clock at all, probably stopped about ten minutes after it left the showroom.

Wiring the clock and radio to work takes some basic electronic knowledge and you will probably have to replace the wires for both. The radio can be taken apart and any faulty parts replaced; and the same goes for the clock if you have one.

Books are available on how repair a radio and a clock and most electronic stores have components for both. It may take some doing to get that clock back into action, but the radio should be fairly simple. Car radios from most vintage eras were not that complicated.

Vintage cars usually have crank up windows, push out "fly windows" and manual seats that are moved forward and back by pulling a lever and using your legs to scoot the seat up or back. Unlike cars today, cars prior to the 1950s did not have "power" windows that operate electronically or power seats that, with the push of a button, move back or forth.

Most of the electronic equipment in vintage cars consisted of a radio, clock (that never really worked if it even had one), and lights. To get any of these things to work, you need a little bit of electronic knowledge.

But don't be too discouraged if you don't have any electronics or electrical knowledge. You may just find a few videos on YouTube that give you a basic breakdown on what you need to get up to speed. Who knows: by the time you get to reading this, I may have a YouTube video on my channel showing you just how to do it.

A Quick Pointer

A store like Radio Shack has nearly everything you need to get that vintage radio working again. The employees on staff are helpful and knowledgeable. If you take the radio in, they should be able to help you find the parts you need.

In the next chapter, "*MODELS ARE MUCH, MUCH EASIER*," we'll begin to reassemble your project.

CHAPTER TEN
MODELS ARE MUCH, MUCH EASIER

Models of your vintage automobile are much, much easier to assemble than reassembling your life sized project. That's a given. There have been times that I thought, "What in the world am I doing?" and considered quitting. I've even thought, "I should have just gone to the store and bought a couple of car models." Maybe a particular part of your project will frustrate you, but don't give up. Once you've worked it out you'll be so glad you hung in there.

Before you begin reassembling your car, you need to make sure that everything works. Test the lights; crank over the engine; check your brakes (which should be new, including new drums or rotors). Once you're satisfied that everything is in good working order, you can begin to reassemble your vehicle.

Another thing you want to do is go over your notes from your composition notebook and the photos that you took of your vehicle as you went along. This is the payoff to your diligence with the photo and notes system I recommended for you; especially if your project has taken you months to complete (or in some cases, a year or two). It will bring back to memory how you removed a particular part, and often, if an item came out in a special way, it may need to be replaced in the same way, but in reverse. If you took photos and careful notes, you will be grateful that you did. Trust me on this one.

Begin by putting the interior back together. The seats you set aside before are now ready for reinstallation. Make sure that everything is secure before doing anything else as you do not want to have to remove these again. Then you can continue by putting on the doors.

After that, put on the hood, trunk lid, and any other body pieces appropriate to your make and model. After this is completed, add the chrome as well as any exterior accessories.

Finally, when the car is completely put back together, start it up. If everything has been done correctly, it should start up with no problem.

If you notice that something is not quite right in the car after you have reassembled it, remember that no one is perfect, and even with the item that's not quite right, your vintage car is probably a hundred times better off than when you started. You may even feel regrets over *"things I should have done differently."* If that comes up, break out your trusty composition notebook and make some notes at back of your book. Keep your notebook for the next project you undertake because you'll want to pull it out and review this last section before starting in. But just in case you misplace that book later on, transpose your finishing notes to your computer.

If your car works and it looks good on a final inspection all the way around, then you have successfully completed your first restoration project. Well done! Congratulations!

Take some final photos all the way around your project. Open the hood and take pictures of your engine, shoot several of the interior from all angles, etc. Just as you did before you got started on your project, you want to keep these photos as a comparison to what you had before you embarked on this restoration.

Another thing that the photo journaling will do for you, is not only provide a running log for your project, but you may also want to use your photos and some of your notes to submit them to one of the magazines, which may choose to insert them in a little feature article. Who knows, they may even pay you a few dollars for your photos.

If you continue on with vintage car restoration, the little tricks you pick up along the way can be documented through your photos and notes, and you may be able to submit them for major features in these magazines.

Now, those who have completed their first restoration are often discouraged when someone has to make a wisecrack about something that they did wrong. Take any criticism in stride and learn from your mistakes. Although we couldn't be very specific in this book because particular details depend upon what kind of car you're restoring, if you followed the basic instructions of this book, you started on a vehicle that was inexpensive and in decent shape to begin with. Being a first project for you will mean that if you continue, you will only get better at this. Be proud of the fact that you've done something that many have never even thought of attempting.

What is important is that you enjoyed working on your project and that you completed it. While some people enjoy competing in certain shows for prizes with their "perfectly" restored cars, others just enjoy being able to say that they did this themselves.

A Quick Pointer

Be proud of your accomplishment. You took an old car and got it to run and look good when driving on the road. Not everyone can say that they done that. Now that you have learned how to perform this extensive restoration work, you can continue to work to improve your craft.

In the next chapter, "*YA GOTTA 4-1-1 BEFORE IT GETS TO 9-1-1*," we'll take a look at where to get help in times of need.

CHAPTER ELEVEN

YA GOTTA 4-1-1 BEFORE IT GETS TO 9-1-1

During the course of your restoration project, you are bound to run into a snag or two... or three... or fifty. This is natural, especially for your first project. This is why it is so important to network with other restoration enthusiasts. As much as possible, get your information first (4-1-1) before it gets to be an emergency (9-1-1).

To some, vintage car restoration is a great hobby. To others it is more than just a hobby or craft; it is a whole way of life. There are people who are completely committed to auto restoration and spend most of their weekends at auto shows. Either way, there are folks out there who will appreciate your interest in auto restoration and will be more than happy to help. And whether it is preliminary information, or help in a particular restoration emergency, you'll want to tap into these resources.

Thanks to the Internet, there are even more ways for those who are embarking on their first restoration project to get help. Before beginning your project, check out the following:

Your Local Library. There are dozens of books at your library on car repair and body work. Best of all, the library is free, as long as you live in an area that has one and you have not been banned for too many overdue books. ☺

Meet-Up Groups. Go to a local "meet-up" for car enthusiasts. This is an easy way to find others who share your interests, who also live in the same area. Meet up groups can be found on the Internet if you go to MeetUp.com. If there is not a meet up group in your city, town or neighborhood, you might want to start one. Although you can find information online, if you join a local group, you can actually borrow tools from other restorers and save money on renting or purchasing equipment.

Online Forums. There are hundreds of websites dedicated to vehicle restoration. Join them. You can find just about any answer to any question by looking online. Most car enthusiasts are only too glad to share their knowledge. Introduce yourself to others and become part of the community.

Blogging. Start a blog using Blogger.com or WordPress.com (or both). Since you are documenting your restoration project with your photos and composition notebook, you can post your photos and your notes online daily with your blog. By keeping the comment section open, people who know something of the restoration process can help you with tips and tricks of the trade. In the forums (mentioned above), your profile can contain your blog address and you can invite those you meet on the forums to read your blog. The interaction you get from the blog as they see your photos may provide you a wealth of information to complete your project. Additionally, search the web for blogs that provide articles on vintage auto restoration. Subscribe to receive updates if that's available. Interact with the blog owner via the comments section.

Auto Shops. Visit your local auto parts dealer and see if they have any advice they can lend. They may have worked on  vintage autos and can recommend products or a store. And don't forget to ask your shop teacher at school. Often, auto shop teachers in local high schools and community colleges know many of the local shop owners and managers.

Classic Car Association. Join an association where you can get help from the members. You may have to pay a fee for this, but in exchange, you will get newsletters and information on where to get the best deals on parts as well as places to show your car once it is finished.

Magazines. Subscribe to magazines for auto restoration enthusiasts. In addition to learning new tips and techniques for restoring your car, you can also find ads for the ever growing parts industry.

eBay. Check out the deals on used books on eBay and Amazon for car restoration. Sometimes these books can be found at a discount off of the regular price. You may also be able to find the original manual for your car online.

Classic Car Shows. Attend classic car shows in your area and talk to the owners of the cars. People who attend these shows have most likely been restoring automobiles for quite some time. They are extremely proud of their craft and eager to talk about it with anyone who wants to listen. Be willing to listen and learn from them. You may even find a mentor.

Local Body Shop. If you really run into a snag while working on the body of the car, talk to the owner of your local body shop and see if he or one of his employees would be willing to help you out on the side for a bit of cash (if the financial resource isn't a burden to you). This applies for the mechanical aspect, as well. If you are really in a bind and cannot do something, ask for help. More than likely, it will cost you less if you pay someone than if you keep attempting to do the job yourself with little or no success.

Professional Restoration Shops. These can be found online. Although they are in the business of doing this for a living and will scoff at any amateur who attempts to do this in their garage, typically they are willing to lend an ear and give you some advice.

As with anything, the more knowledge and resources you have, the better off you are, and will be. Look for resources and knowledge wherever you can and continue to learn about this craft so that you can improve your skills.

A Quick Pointer

Keep in mind that you are working on restoring an old car. You're not performing brain surgery on a family member. While you should take a considerable amount of pride in anything you do, keep the entire project in perspective and don't feel like a failure if you have to ask for help.

In the next chapter, "**_TLC_**," we'll take a look at your car's "aftercare."

CHAPTER TWELVE
TLC

Your restored car should be kept in a heated garage and covered during the winter. You've spent a lot of time and money working on your car and you want to make sure that it stays in excellent condition. The aftercare for your auto restoration project will require some Tender Loving Care.

If you live in an area where it is warm and dry most of the time, like Arizona, you can take the  car out throughout the year without a problem. If you live in a climate where there is snow and ice, you will not want to take the car out during the winter months. The salt used for winter roads will greatly damage your car body and undercarriage.

As with any car, you should be sure to change the oil, rotate the tires and perform a tune up of the engine every year. Start up your car periodically in the winter months and make sure you keep the gas tank filled to avoid moisture build up.

Any car will respond to such treatment by continuing to run smoothly. By treating your car with care, you will be able to enjoy it for years to come.

A Quick Pointer

Besides the composition notebook you used for your restoration, I strongly recommend that you get another composition notebook as part of your aftercare. On the first couple of pages make a list of all the routine maintenance that is recommended for your car from the owner's manual; such as tune up, oil change, differential fluid change, etc. In the pages following, provide a single page for each item and then write the completion date and odometer reading at the top of the page. Whenever routine maintenance is accomplished, write down the date and odometer reading when each maintenance task is performed. More than a mere record, it will help you to troubleshoot problems should they arise.

In the next chapter, "*WHEN YOU COME TO A FORK IN THE ROAD, TAKE IT*," we'll look at Professional Car Restoration.

CHAPTER THIRTEEN
WHEN YOU COME TO A FORK IN THE ROAD, TAKE IT

Professional car restoration is often used by people who collect antique or vintage cars and want them restored in pristine condition. Professional car restoration often strives for the *Concours d'Elegance* as this is the highest level of restoration. Cars who meet this degree of restoration *look better* than when they left the showroom.

Although it is difficult for an amateur to achieve Concours d'Elegance when it comes to car restoration, it is not impossible. Much will depend, however, on how much money you are willing to sink into the project, and how much tenacity you have as a restorer.

Collectors usually send their vintage autos to a professional restorer to have it brought up to the highest possible standard. Tens of thousands of dollars are spent in order to make this happen. Professional car restoration employs state of the art technology and equipment to literally take a car apart and put it back together again.

By this standard, your first project would be considered the work of an amateur. And though you can learn much from those things you have studied from manuals and courses offered in auto repair and restoration, you're not in "professional" standing, at least not yet (and I'll mention something of that a bit later). Remember to keep the project in perspective. This is a car that you are working on; it's not a matter of life or death. If you have the time and the desire to do the job right, you achieve perfection... or at least Concours d'Elegance.

Most people who have been restoring cars for a while and selling them for profit consider themselves "professional car restorers." Technically, this is so. They are making a profit from their craft; that earns them the title of doing it "professionally." These people can be excellent mentors to those who are just starting out.

There are a number of websites on the Internet featuring professional car restoration services. If you happen across a site that claims that it is "impossible" for amateurs to do a good job and that to achieve quality, you have to take your car to them, don't be offended. You wouldn't expect them to market it any other way would you? Car restoration is their livelihood and if they admitted just anyone could do it they'd be out of business. Don't let that discourage you when you read it, especially when you run across a particular snag in the process that's giving you trouble.

If you follow the tips outlined in this book, you will be able to restore your car. You need to have patience and the desire to learn— nothing more; nothing less... well, except for maybe money for parts; but that goes without saying.

Now, I mentioned earlier that you are not a professional restorer... "at least not yet." This book was specifically written for  young adults; in other words, you. And not only do I *NOT* want to discourage you from car restoration as a profession, I'd actually like to *encourage* you. Perhaps you've found that you have a particular knack for this craft. If you do, then why don't you pursue it? That's right. Go for it. You have a love for cars and you've completed your first project, do you still have a passion for going out and starting up another project right away? Then consider doing this as a profession.

I wanted to be a Navy diver since I was seven years old and I got to do just that. I spent a decade and a half in the U.S. Navy doing what I loved and fulfilling a lifelong dream. Not everyone can say that they grew up to do exactly what they dreamed of doing. And it wasn't something that just dropped into my lap. I wasn't the strongest swimmer nor was I the most athletic of young men. But perseverance and hard work opened the doors for me. I became a strong swimmer, a strong runner and an athletic individual.

If vintage auto restoration is something you'd like to do for a living, don't let anyone stop you.

 But if it isn't, that's okay too. If it was fun and rewarding, but not something that you would do for a living, then let me encourage you to follow whatever career dream you have. If you purchased this book, or someone else purchased this for you as a gift, and if reading this did nothing else for you except to tell you that you can be whatever you want to be, and you were encouraged and motivated by it, then it was worth reading to this point, wasn't it?

Yogi Berra, the famous catcher for the New York Yankees, and later manager for the team, used to say things that were strange but endearing. One of them was used as the title of this chapter. By using a "Yogi-ism" for our chapter title, it's my little way of saying, don't be confined to the conventional choices that seem to be before you, left or right... just take it...

Follow your dreams. Pursue your goals. Be all that you can be.

A Quick Pointer

Ignore the anti-amateur dialog on the professional car restoration sites and don't let it dissuade you from learning this craft. What one man can do— so can another.

In the next chapter, "*IT'S SHOWTIME*," we'll take a look at Classic Car Shows.

CHAPTER FOURTEEN
IT'S SHOWTIME!

If you join the Classic Car Association, you will be entitled to newsletters that will give you an opportunity to find out where the auto shows are in your area.

For your first venture, you may want to join a car club in the area and exhibit your car at the neighborhood car show. Just  about every neighborhood has an exhibit like one of these. You can usually enter the exhibit for free. There are no prizes and no fee for anyone to take a look. You simply sit there with the hood of the car open as well as the doors and allow people to see your car. You have to constantly remind kids not to touch.

If you have ever been to one of these local shows, you know how it operates. You can spend the day chatting with other car enthusiasts who will give you constructive criticism about your car, whether you ask or not. It's a great way to make a few new friends.

After you have gotten a bit more confident in your car restoration abilities, you may choose to participate in an antique car club show. There are antique car clubs located all over the United States. You can find these easily enough on the Internet, however, I'll provide you with some web addresses for some of the major ones just below.

Many of the antique car clubs have monthly shows in which auto restorers compete with one another for prizes. Most of the prizes are non-monetary. Plaques and trophies are often awarded in different categories.

When you have reached the level of *Concours d'Elegance*, you can participate in one of the large antique car shows that occur each year in the United States. Some of the most popular car shows are held annually at Meadow Brook, Michigan. Check them out on the Internet at

www.meadowbrookconcours.org

Another exciting venue for car restoration enthusiasts is the annual antique car exhibition and auction held at Hilton Head, South Carolina. These are some of the top shows in the country. In addition to exhibition, some car owners auction their cars to the highest bidder. Their web address is

www.hhiconcours.com

One of the oldest car show events is the Stowe Car Show in Vermont. This has been held every year for over fifty years. The Stowe Car Show is one of the most beloved classic car shows in the United States. You can find them at

www.gostowe.com/antique-car-show

Car restoration enthusiasts travel each year to Vermont to participate in this show. Prizes are given in several different categories, including for interior design, exterior excellence and overall restoration quality.

All types of vintage cars can enter this show. Here you will see everything from muscle cars of the 1970s to pre-WWI veteran cars.

The most prestigious classic car show in the United States is the Concours d'Elegance at Pebble Beach. This features the *crème de le crème* of all restored classic cars. The prizes for the show range from $200,000 to $400,000. There are prizes for the street show as well, in which cars are judged on how well they run. You can find more information about this great show at **www.pebblebeachconcours.net**

Most classic auto shows have requirements for exhibition. Take a look around and see if you can find one that will suit the type of car that you have restored. There are some that only feature cars from the 1950s, while others only want pre-WWII cars. There are classic car shows for just about every era.

If you have restored one of the fun cars from the 1960s or 1970s, you can also find a car show in which to exhibit your car. Many people are watching the cars that they grew up with being turned into "classics" because of the interest in "retro." Young people today admire the 1970s and 1980s and this era is becoming more and more popular, including even the "tacky" or everyday economy cars of the era, such as the AMC Gremlin and Pacer.

The nice thing about joining a car club is that you become a member of a community. You will get to meet with other people who are also interested in restoring cars and you can learn different techniques and tips from them.

The next chapter, "*PARTS AND POINTERS*," will cover where to buy parts and will include pointers for restoration.

CHAPTER *FIFTEEN*
PARTS AND POINTERS

 **Parts**

There are many different ways to get the parts that you need to restore your car. One of the best places to go is to the Internet. You can do a quick search on vintage parts for the type of car that you are restoring and will probably come up with a lot of sites.

The best ways to find parts for your restoration project include the following:

- ✓ Internet auction sites
- ✓ Vintage car parts websites
- ✓ Swap meets with other car enthusiasts
- ✓ Junk yards (this can be difficult if you are restoring a popular model)

- ✓ Restoration shops
- ✓ Auto parts store
- ✓ Magazine ads

You can find many different portals on the Internet for those who are interested in antique car restoration. These will direct you to anything you need.

Thanks to the Internet, vintage car restoration has never been easier. By joining an online community and using this valuable tool, you not only get assistance from other people who also enjoy this craft, but you will also find the parts you need to make your restoration a success.

 **Pointers**

Before starting any restoration, read the following pointers to make sure that your project goes well.

Protect Your Paint Job

When you are re-assembling your restored car, the last thing that you want to do is to damage the new paint job. When assembling the bumpers, hood, trunk like doors, windshield, etc, there are ways that can help you avoid damage to the paint:

- ✓ Use shims when installing the fenders so that you do not damage the paint and so it remains flush with the body of the car;
- ✓ Use new hinge mounts if keeping the original hood and trunk lid as the mounts tend to get rusty and may make it difficult to close flush with the body of the car;
- ✓ Replace all weather stripping on the windows and windshield before putting them back on the car.

Emblems and Trim

Make sure that you use the correct emblems and trim that came with the car. These can be purchased at the same place where you purchase original parts. Do not allow your car to go unfinished without the necessary emblems and trim.

Getting Your Car Ready for Paint

After you have used a power sander to sand down your car, make sure that you wash and dry it thoroughly before applying primer. You can also use an air compressor to dry of your parts before applying primer; but as mentioned earlier in the book, use the magnetic as well. Use an approved solvent as well to take care of any moisture. Automotive tape can be used to tape up anything that you do not want painted.

Yellowed Headlights

If you are fortunate enough to have the original headlights on your car, they may have gotten yellow with age. This is normal when a car is older. There are several different methods for getting the yellow out of the headlights and restoring them to new.

Some people claim using toothpaste will get the headlights back to pristine condition. There is a kit made available by the manufacturers of *Permatex* that is made specifically for restoring the yellowed headlights. It can be found at your local auto parts store.

Small Rust Spots

Small rust spots can be rubbed out with an abrasive pad. Larger rust spots will have to be removed with a power tool, such as a power sander that has an abrasive head.

Equipment Rental

One of the reasons you should join a car club is to find the best places to rent equipment in your area. Most of the equipment, such as the power sprayer, power sander, and the detailer, are very expensive to purchase. You can save money by renting this equipment at a rental store or borrowing the equipment from friends in your club.

Wash and Wax by Hand

Do not take your car to an automatic car wash. Most of them have wire brushes that can damage your car. Take care of your car by hand washing and waxing it. Protect the new paint and body that it took you so long to create.

Use an Air compressor

When you have washed the car and want to make sure that it is absolutely dry, use an air compressor to be certain that all of the water is out of the car. The last thing you need is for the car to be damaged by moisture.

Protect Yourself

One cannot say enough about this topic. Make sure you wear a respirator when you are working on your car as well as goggles. Use gloves and respirator when working with solvents and chemicals.

SAFETY FIRST— ALWAYS!

Use a Car Cover

Even in a heated garage, treat the object of your affection, your restored car, as a cherished piece of property. Invest in a car cover that will keep it warm, even in the heated garage. The cover will help protect your vehicle if someone should brush up against the body carelessly. Get a quality cover with a gentle lining.

Brake Shoes and Drums (or Pads/Rotors)

Replace the brake shoes and turn the drums of your car on a regular basis. If you only replace the shoes without turning the drums, the brake replacements will wear out quicker and work less efficiently because of grooves cut into the drum. Most of the older cars use shoes and drums; although you may be working on a car that uses brake pads and rotors. When the drums have been worn to their minimum thickness, replace them.

The same will apply for cars using brake pads and rotors. Have the rotors turned until they cannot be turned any longer.

Save the Chrome

If you are restoring a car from the 1950s, do what you can to repair the chrome. Chrome is very expensive to replace and repairing the chrome is much cheaper. There are certain chrome shops that will do this work for you, or you can attempt to do it yourself. There are dips that you can use to clean the chrome, but they are expensive very expensive.

Replace Wiring

Most of the electrical wiring in your car may be shot. Unless you are a skilled electrician, you may be better off replacing the wires instead of trying to repair what's left.

Wooden Parts

Some cars have wooden dashboards or panels. Wood restoration is similar to metal restoration. The wood should be stripped and varnished so that it looks like new.

Invest in a Floor Jack

If you do not have a good jack in your garage, now may be a good time to get one. You can work a lot easier under the car with a proper lift, and it is much safer as well.

Outsourcing Your Work

If you need help, do not hesitate to farm out a piece of work to a professional. In most cases, this will be cheaper than if you try to do it yourself and have to repeat the process over and over again until you get it right.

Replace Wiper Blades and Spark Plugs

This would seem to be a common sense point, but you would be surprised at how many people attempt to restore a vintage car and try to clean the spark plugs instead of simply replacing them. This is one thing that it really pays to replace rather than repair.

Take the windshield wiper blades off of the car before putting the new blades in so you do not scratch your car.

Car Kits

There are many different car kits available both online and at your auto parts store that can help you with the mechanical aspect of your restoration. Car kits are made for most types of cars on the market and offer everything you need to rebuild an engine or transmission. You are sometimes better off buying a kit than trying to buy each part yourself.

Clean the Exhaust Pipe

Don't forget to clean and polish the exhaust pipe of the car. This can easily be removed when you are removing the engine. You want this to shine just like anything else on your car. Moreover, ensure that you clean the undercarriage of the car as well.

Don't Forget the Trunk

Trunks are usually lined with a carpet like substance today. Years ago, trunks were not lined. Make sure that you restore the interior of the trunk as well as the body. Although it is not normally opened during car shows, you will want to have the car totally restored.

Well, you've made it to the end of the book. We'll say, "So long," with the last chapter, "*JOB WELL DONE!*"

CHAPTER SIXTEEN
JOB WELL DONE!

No matter how you got there, the car of your dreams now belongs to you. You have lovingly restored it to as close to its original condition as possible. You should be proud to show it off to others and take it for a spin on the street.

Don't allow others to stop you from what you want to do with your car restoration project (and as I mentioned earlier, don't let anyone stop you with what you want to do with your life). Although the standards of car restoration call for trying to restore the car to the original condition, if you want to do something unique, feel fee. The car is yours.

When your car is finished, take a special joy in what you've done, even if it didn't turn out "perfect." Very few of us ever get to "perfect," and certainly not on our first try. It is more important that you enjoyed the experience of restoring your car.

 If you decide that you want to restore another car, after this experience you should have spotted your particular strengths and weaknesses. In fact, at each stage of the process you discovered a bit more about what you were better at than others. Use that knowledge to your advantage. If, for example, you are better on the mechanical side, you should buy something that looks decent on the outside but does not run. If, on the other hand, you have a knack for body work, then you should look for a car that runs but is not much to look at. This will save you a lot of money on your next project purchase.

Additionally, it is very important to befriend others when you are working on this hobby. Although you may enjoy your time to yourself when working on your car, you will still need the knowledge and support of other people during the course of your restoration.

Custom Classic Cars

Restoring your classic car can lead to a whole new world. It can give you an excellent hobby  that you will enjoy for years to come, open up doors for new friendships, and even earn you prizes and money at shows.

In reality, you've probably not yet started on your project, which is natural for anyone. You wanted to get all you could out of this book first. Nevertheless, if you are using this as a quick reference on a couple of points that I've made, it will be close by when you have completed your project. In that case, "Well Done!"

If you're starting a project or completed one, stop by our blog and tell us how your project is going. We can post some of your photos and we invite you to submit articles on the progress of your vehicle restoration. Check it out at

http://car-custom-classics.info

Jon J. Cardwell is a wretched sinner saved by God's free and sovereign grace. He lives in Anniston, Alabama with his wife, Lisa, his daughter, Rachel, and his mother-in-law, Virginia. He is the pastor at Sovereign Grace Baptist Church in Anniston after having ministered as a missionary and as a missionary-pastor in the Philippines, California, and remote bush Alaska.

He is the author of the bestseller, *Christ and Him Crucified*, the CEO of Vayahiy Press, and the founder and overseer of Free Grace Tentmakers. Jon has also held the office of vice-chairman of the national Sovereign Grace Baptist Fellowship (2009-11), and was elected as chairman on September 13, 2011.

His Christianity has been shaped tremendously and influenced deeply by such redeemed sinners as John Bunyan (1628-

1688), Charles H. Spurgeon (1834-1892), John Newton (1725-1807), and Granville Gauldin (1929-).

<u>Some of Jon's other titles include</u>:

Christ and Him Crucified
Lord, Teach Us to Pray
Fullness of the Time
A Puritan Family Devotional
A Pilgrim Family Devotional
A Puritan Bible Primer
PLR Payday
Master Mega Writing

<u>Jon's blogs include</u>:

Justification by Grace
http://justificationbygrace.com
(Sign up for updates and receive FREE eReport, "Three Primary Obstacles to the Gospel in the West & What to Do About It"); or go to http://gospelobstacles.com

Preaching Christ Crucified
http://preachingchristcrucified.com
(Sign up for updates and receive FREE eReport, "The Shroud of Turin: Holy or Hoax?"); or go to http://lyingwonders.com

Free Grace Tentmakers
http://incomesupplementnow.com
(Sign up for updates and receive FREE eReport, "Internet Marketing from A to Z"); or go to http://firstlittlepiggy.com

Ministry websites include:

Jon J. Cardwell Online
http://jonjcardwell.net

Vayahiy Press
http://vayahiypress.com

SermonAudio
www.sermonaudio.com/vayahiy

Social media includes:

Facebook
www.facebook.com/jon.cardwell

Twitter
www.twitter.com/vayahiy

LinkedIn
www.linkedin.com/in/joncardwell

CPSIA information can be obtained
at www.ICGtesting.com
Printed in the USA
BVHW040201100322
631128BV00007BA/169